Tyrannosaurus Was a Beast

Dinosaur Poems by JACK PRELUTSKY
illustrated by ARNOLD LOBEL

A Mulberry Paperback Book
New York

To the New Mexico Museum of Natural History

Watercolors, dry mark, and a black pen were used for the illustrations. The text type is Veljovic.
Text copyright © 1988 by Jack Prelutsky. Illustrations copyright © 1988 by Arnold Lobel. All rights
reserved. No part of this book may be reproduced or utilized in any form or by any means, electronic
or mechanical, including photocopying, recording, or by any information storage or retrieval system,
without permission in writing from the Publisher. Inquiries should be addressed to Greenwillow
Books, a division of William Morrow & Company, Inc., 1350 Avenue of the Americas, New York,
New York 10019. Printed in the United States of America.

The Library of Congress has cataloged the Greenwillow Books edition of *Tyrannosaurus Was a Beast*
as follows: Prelutsky, Jack. Tyrannosaurus was a beast. Summary: A collection of humorous poems
about dinosaurs. ISBN 0-688-06442-6 ISBN 0-688-06443-4 (lib. bdg.) 1. Dinosaurs—Juvenile poetry.
2. Children's poetry, American. [1. Dinosaurs—Poetry. 2. American poetry] I. Lobel, Arnold, ill.
II. Title.   PS3566.R36T97 1988 811'.54 87-25131

10 9 8
First Mulberry Edition, 1992
ISBN 0-688-11569-1

THE DINOSAURS

TYRANNOSAURUS
Late Cretaceous
Western North America
50′ long; 18½′ tall

BRACHIOSAURUS
Middle Jurassic-Early Cretaceous
Western United States, Africa, Europe
75-85′ long; 40′ tall

LEPTOPTERYGIUS
Triassic-Cretaceous
Northern Hemisphere
40-45′ long; 12½′ high

STEGOSAURUS
Jurassic
Colorado, Utah, Wyoming, parts of Europe
25-30′ long; 11′ tall

DEINONYCHUS
Early Cretaceous
Western United States
10-15′ long; 5′ tall

ANKYLOSAURUS
Cretaceous
Western North America
25-35′ long; 4′ tall

DIPLODOCUS
Late Jurassic-Early Cretaceous
Colorado, Montana, Utah, Wyoming
90′ long; 13′ tall (not including neck)

COELOPHYSIS
Late Triassic
New Mexico, Eastern United States
10′ long; 13′ tall (not including neck)

TRICERATOPS
Late Cretaceous
Western North America
25-30′ long; 9½′ tall

CORYTHOSAURUS
Late Cretaceous
California, Western Canada
25-35′ long; 15′ tall

ALLOSAURUS
Late Jurassic
Africa, Asia, Western North America
35-45′ long; 16½′ tall

IGUANODON
Early Cretaceous
Every continent except Antarctica
25′ long; 15′ tall

QUETZALCOATLUS
Late Cretaceous
Most of North America
40-50′ wingspan; 8′ tall

SEISMOSAURUS
Jurassic
New Mexico
110′ long; 50′ tall

TYRANNOSAURUS

tie-RAN-uh-sawr-us
"Tyrant Lizard"

Tyrannosaurus was a beast
that had no friends, to say the least.
It ruled the ancient out-of-doors,
and slaughtered other dinosaurs.

BRACHIOSAURUS

BRAK-ee-uh-sawr-us
"Arm Lizard"

Brachiosaurus had little to do
but stand with its head in the treetops and chew,
it nibbled the leaves that were tender and green,
it was a perpetual eating machine.

Brachiosaurus was truly immense,
its vacuous mind was uncluttered by sense,
it hadn't the need to be clever and wise,
no beast dared to bother a being its size.

Brachiosaurus was clumsy and slow,
but then, there was nowhere it needed to go,
if Brachiosaurus were living today,
no doubt it would frequently be in the way.

LEPTOPTERYGIUS

lep-toe-ter-IDGE-ee-us
"Partially Finned"

Leptopterygius lived in the ocean,
Leptopterygius swam very fast,
its head was enormous, its fangs were abundant,
its temper ferocious, its appetite vast.

Leptopterygius, big as a city bus,
was an insatiable ichthyosaur,
anything captured by Leptopterygius
never was seen in the sea anymore.

Leptopterygius ate every morsel,
it managed to catch in the long-ago sea,
so I am grateful that Leptopterygius
isn't around to go swimming with me.

STEGOSAURUS

steg-uh-SAWR-us
"Plated Lizard"

Stegosaurus was a creature uncontentious and benign,
and the row of armored plates upon its back
failed to guard its tender belly or protect its flimsy spine—
Stegosaurus often wound up as a snack.

Stegosaurus blundered calmly through the prehistoric scene,
never causing any other creature woe,
its brain was somewhat smaller than the average nectarine—
Stegosaurus vanished many years ago.

DEINONYCHUS

die-no-NYKE-us
"Terrible Claw"

Deinonychus was named for its terrible claw,
Deinonychus was savage and cunning,
it pounced on its victims and swallowed them raw,
before they had even stopped running.

Ferocity was its predominant trait,
its habits were purely predacious,
it ate what it caught, and it caught what it ate
in the days of the early Cretaceous.

Large dinosaurs quaked when this monster came near
to stuff them inside of its belly,
how fortunate then, that it's no longer here
to eat us like cream cheese and jelly.

ANKYLOSAURUS

an-kile-uh-SAWR-us
"Stiffened Lizard"

Clankity Clankity Clankity Clank!
Ankylosaurus was built like a tank,
its hide was a fortress as sturdy as steel,
it tended to be an inedible meal.

It was armored in front, it was armored behind,
there wasn't a thing on its minuscule mind,
it waddled about on its four stubby legs,
nibbling on plants with a mouthful of pegs.

Ankylosaurus was best left alone,
its tail was a cudgel of gristle and bone,
Clankity Clankity Clankity Clank!
Ankylosaurus was built like a tank.

DIPLODOCUS

di-PLOD-uh-kus
"Double Beam"

Diplodocus plodded along on the trail
on four massive thundering feet,
it had a long neck, and a serpentine tail,
and Diplodocus plodded along long ago,
Diplodocus plodded along.

Diplodocus feasted from morning till night,
it did almost nothing but eat,
it couldn't go far without taking a bite,
and Diplodocus plodded along long ago,
Diplodocus plodded along.

Diplodocus needed to stay on its toes,
and watch with its skyscraper eyes,
for it was surrounded by ravenous foes,
and Diplodocus plodded along long ago,
Diplodocus plodded along.

Diplodocus never could move very fast
because of its ponderous size,
it lived long ago, and its time is now past,
and Diplodocus plodded along long ago,
Diplodocus plodded along.

COELOPHYSIS

see-lo-FYS-is
"Hollow Form"

FIE-toe-sore
"Plant Lizard"

Coelophysis was a hunter
with efficient teeth and claws,
it gobbled any animal
that fit between its jaws,
its head was rather narrow,
and its neck and tail were long,
its vision was uncommon,
and its legs were fast and strong.

Coelophysis chewed on lizards,
Coelophysis swallowed ants,
Coelophysis gnawed on mammals,
but it never dined on plants,
Coelophysis stayed attentive,
or a crisis was in store,
and the hunter made a morsel
for a mighty Phytosaur.

TRICERATOPS

try-SAIR-uh-tops
"Three-horned Face"

Triceratops had one short horn,
and two as long as spears,
it dwelled near scores of carnosaurs,
and yet it had no fears.

Triceratops was dangerous,
impervious and strong,
the predators that challenged it
did not last very long.

Triceratops fought valiantly,
and vanquished every foe,
so why it ever disappeared,
nobody seems to know.

CORYTHOSAURUS

ko-RITH-uh-sawr-us
"Helmet Lizard"

Corythosaurus long ago,
wandered to and wandered fro,
ambled in and ambled out,
munching as it went about.

Corythosaurus moved with grace,
it had a duckbill on its face,
it had a helmet on its head,
it could have used some brains instead.

Corythosaurus, short on sense,
had no semblance of defense,
though it did the best it could,
Corythosaurus is gone for good.

ALLOSAURUS

al-uh-SAWR-us
"Different Lizard"

Allosaurus liked to bite,
its teeth were sharp as sabers,
it frequently, with great delight,
made mincemeat of its neighbors.

Allosaurus liked to hunt,
and when it caught its quarry,
it tore it open, back and front,
and never said, "I'm sorry!"

Allosaurus liked to eat,
and using teeth and talons,
it stuffed itself with tons of meat,
and guzzled blood by gallons.

Allosaurus liked to munch,
and kept from growing thinner
by gnawing an enormous lunch,
then rushing off to dinner.

IGUANODON

ig-WAN-o-don
"Iguana-tooth"

Iguanodon, Iguanodon,
whatever made you fade,
you've traveled on, Iguanodon,
we wish you could have stayed.

Iguanodon, Iguanodon,
we've sought you everywhere,
both here and yon, Iguanodon,
but failed to find you there.

Iguanodon, Iguanodon,
you were a gentle kind,
but now you're gone, Iguanodon,
and left your bones behind.

QUETZALCOATLUS

ket-sol-ko-AT-lus

Named after Quetzalcoatl, the Aztec
feathered serpent god

Quetzalcoatlus once mastered the skies,
a reptile in aerodynamic disguise,
its fifty-foot wingspan sustained it aloft,
its takeoffs were nimble, its landings were soft.

Quetzalcoatlus, an animate plane
glided and soared over ancient terrain,
the largest and mightiest creature that flew,
it did very well without pilot or crew.

SEISMOSAURUS

size-mo-SAWR-us
"Earthshaking Lizard"

Seismosaurus was enormous,
Seismosaurus was tremendous,
Seismosaurus was prodigious,
Seismosaurus was stupendous.

Seismosaurus was titanic,
Seismosaurus was colossal,
Seismosaurus now is nothing
but a monumental fossil.

WHEN THE DINOSAURS LIVED

PALEOZOIC	MESOZOIC			CENOZOIC
	TRIASSIC	JURASSIC	CRETACEOUS	

225 million   190 million   135 million   65 million   present
years ago   years ago   years ago   years ago